101
So Bad,
They're Good

Irish Dad
Jokes

Elias Hill

Other Dad Jokes Books by Elias Hill You Might Enjoy:

101 So Bad, They're Good Dad Jokes

101 Dad Jokes: Christmas Edition

Dad Jokes - Assault With A Dad-ly Weapon: Official Dad Gift Idea

More 101 So Bad, They're Good Dad Jokes

101 So Bad, They're Good Dad Jokes (Volume 2)

Dad Jokes? I Think You Mean Rad Jokes!: 101 New Dad Jokes For The New Year

101 So Bad, They're Good Dad Jokes: Golf Edition

What do you call an Irish computer virus?

O'Malleyware!

Two Irishmen were about to get into a fight. One drew a line in the dirt and said, "If you cross this line, I'll clatter you in the jaw."

That was the punchline.

I made a new friend in Ireland.

Oh, really?

No, O'Reilly.

What happened to the rainbow after he robbed a bank?

He got prism for light.

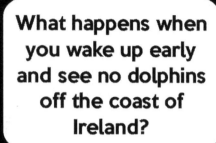

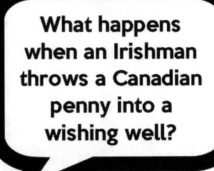

What organizational sport do leprechauns like best?

Little League.

An Irishman wanted to start making his own hard liquor,
but he heard it was a whiskey business.

I'd borrow some money from a leprechaun...

but they're always a little short!

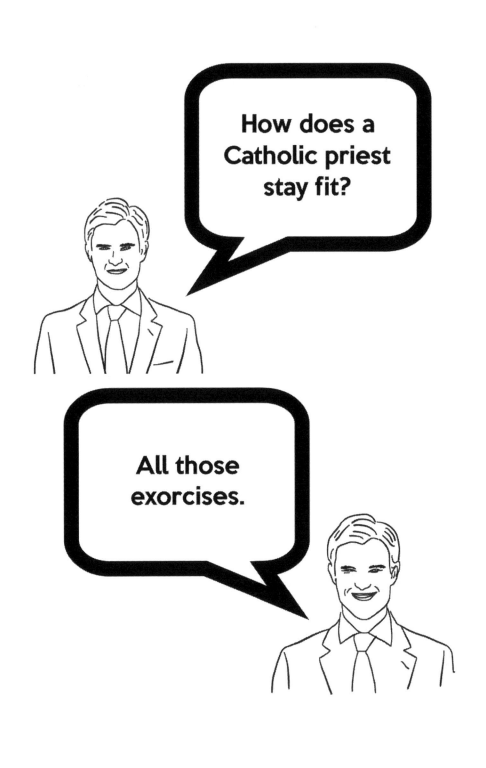

Our son set the pub on fire.

That's arson!

Yes, *our* son.

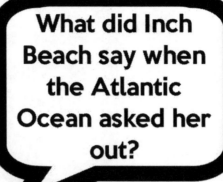

Did you hear about the Irish fossil they found in South America?

It's like a Brazilian years old.

Who is the patron saint of email?

Saint Francis of a cc.

How many bones are in the average Irishman's hand?

A handful.

What happened to the Irishman who started an argument with his wife while riding in an elevator?

He was wrong on so many levels.

The Irishman snored so loudly...

it frightened everyone in the car he was driving.

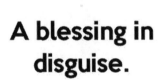

An Irish immigration officer may not always agree with you...

but he can see where you're coming from.

Why did the Irishman get gold teeth?

He wanted to put his money where his mouth was.

I never believed my Irish friend would steal from his road working job.
But then I started to see the signs.

Why was the
Blarney Stone
angry?

He was taken
for granite.

A landlord wanted to speak to an Irish tenant about how high his heating bills were.

"Sure," the Irishman replied, "my door's always open."

Why did the congregation ask the old priest to leave?

They were in search of greener pastors.

What do you call a Dwayne Johnson impersonator?

A sham Rock!

Hey, there's a flock of Irish cows.

Herd of cows.

Of course I've heard of cows, I just pointed out a flock of them.

An Irishman walks into a bar with a piece of cement under his arm and says to the bartender,

"A whiskey please, and one for the road."

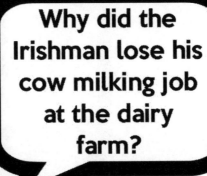

Did you hear about the nun who never did her laundry?

She had a filthy habit.

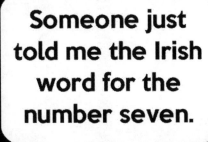

Made in the USA
Columbia, SC
20 February 2019